This is a true story.

In the foothills of the Colorado Rockies during the summer of '86, the shrill ring of a telephone woke Kendra and Marty Homola out of a sound sleep. The caller had seen a mother buffalo struggling to give birth. As the Homolas hurried to help, Cruiser and Mickey waited at the gate.

Nickel

with love,
Nancy Savage

The Baby Buffalo
Who Thought He Was a Dog

by Nancy Savage ❖ illustrations by Kathy Parks

To Noodles 'n Doodles
A nickel from the sale of each book
is donated to a literacy program.
N. S. & K. P.

Library of Congress
Catalog Card Number
98-96917
Nickel: The Baby Buffalo Who Thought He Was a Dog
by Nancy Savage: illustrated by Kathy Parks
typography: Sue McCollough
Summary: tells the true story of Nickel, an orphaned bison calf,
the adventures leading to his dehorning, and his triumphant survival.
ISBN 0-9669130-1-9 (PBK.)
I. Buffalo, Colorado history
[1. Colorado history 2. Denver Mountain Parks 3. Wildlife care 4. Imprinting]
II. Title. Colorado 1999
Teacher's Guide
ISBN 0-9669130-2-7

Savage Parks Press
25958 Genesee Trail Road
Golden, Colorado 80401

The truck zoomed into the buffalo compound. They found the mother buffalo in a secluded gully, but it was too late to save her.

Kendra pointed at two big brown eyes peering out beside the mother. "Look, Marty, the calf is still alive!"

The calf caught sight of them, leaped in surprise, and wobbled toward Kendra on unsteady legs.

Marty watched his wife pet the calf. As caretaker of a buffalo ranch in Genesee Park, he knew that none of the buffalo would feed an orphaned calf. If it were left here, it would die.

It was August 2, Kendra's birthday. "Here's your present," Marty grinned, as he hoisted the 70-pound newborn into the back of the pickup.

Kendra climbed in back too and cuddled the trembling calf as Marty drove back to the ranch house.

As the truck pulled up, Jason bounded out of the house. He could hardly believe his eyes as his dad placed the new family pet in the corral.

"What will we feed him, Dad?"

Marty called the zoo for advice. The zookeeper urged him to make the long drive to the zoo for a special milk formula.

Kendra lay down in the dirt beside the hungry newborn and cuddled him until Marty's return. "C'mere Mickey," she coaxed her dog. "This young'un needs a bath." Mickey licked and licked till the calf was thoroughly washed. Newborn animals imprint. They believe that the first living being they see is what they are. Although the little bison identified at first with Kendra, after his first bath he knew who he *really* was. He was a *dog!*

When Marty returned with frozen milk from the zoo's mother buffalo, Kendra thawed it in the microwave, while Jason found an empty two-liter pop bottle. Marty filled the bottle and added a sheep nipple to the top.

The starving orphan gulped and guzzled a full gallon of the delicious warm milk. Then he curled up in the corral, gave a loud burp, and dozed off for a long nap in his new home.

"He needs a special name. What should we call him?" asked Jason. Marty pulled a buffalo head nickel out of his pocket and tossed the coin to Jason.

"Let's call him Nickel."

Every two hours round the clock the family took turns feeding Nickel his bottle. Kendra rubbed his back and tenderly caressed the soft furry spot above his eyes. She rocked him back and forth, her sweet-talk and lullabies soothing him to sleep. The motherless calf needed lots of care. But they all agreed Nickel was worth it.

Except for Mickey.

Nickel loved to lick Mickey's long, soft ears, but Nickel's tongue felt like scratchy sandpaper. Mickey growled and snapped at Nickel, but it was no use. Poor Mickey finally just accepted it. From then on her ears were always soaking wet.

During the day the pets napped together on the back porch. At first Cruiser and Mickey welcomed their new snuggling buddy. But it wasn't long before the growing newcomer took up all the room! The poor dogs slunk into the house to find another place to nap.

When the dogs went inside, Nickel tried to follow. But he was too big to go through the dog-door. Early one morning Kendra gasped as Nickel burst into the kitchen, slid across the waxed floor, and pinned her against the sink, demanding his bottle. He had turned the doorknob with his *mouth!*

The dogs played with Nickel every day. Their favorite sport was chasing cars along the fence. One autumn day tourists from New York drove past the ranch. The four-legged trio tore off in pursuit — dogs barking, Nickel's tail straight up in the air.

"Hey, Myrtle, look at that *dawg!* Get me the camera!" the driver shouted to his wife. He pulled into the yard and slammed on the brakes. "Hey, Mister," he called to Marty. "We recognize these other breeds, but what kind of dawg is *this?*"

"A really *big* one," Marty grinned.

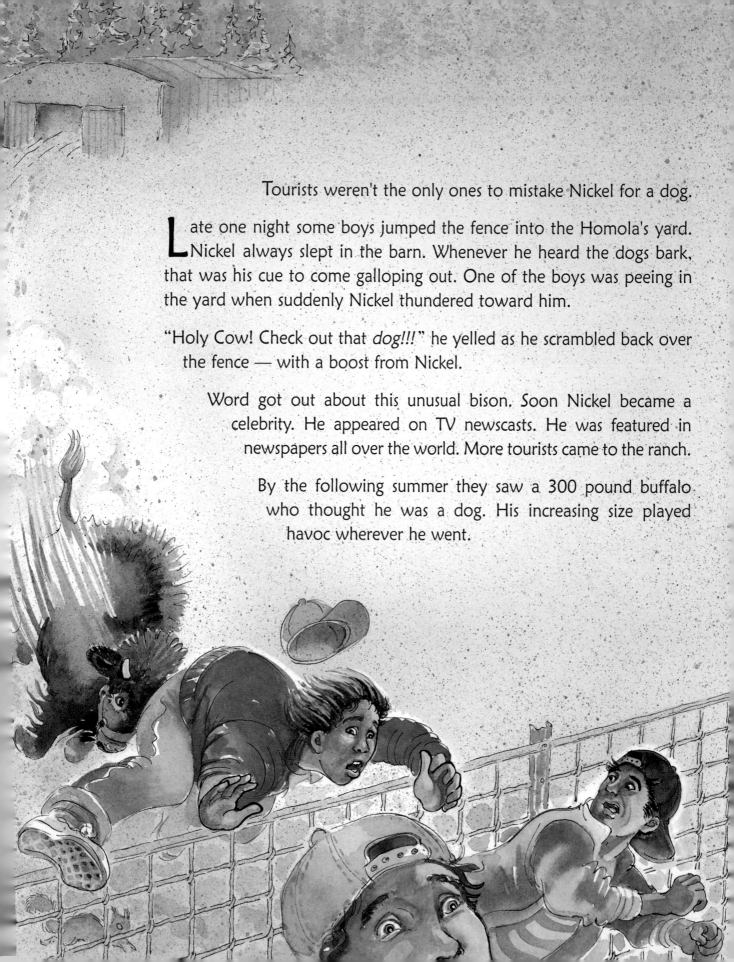

Tourists weren't the only ones to mistake Nickel for a dog.

Late one night some boys jumped the fence into the Homola's yard. Nickel always slept in the barn. Whenever he heard the dogs bark, that was his cue to come galloping out. One of the boys was peeing in the yard when suddenly Nickel thundered toward him.

"Holy Cow! Check out that *dog!!!*" he yelled as he scrambled back over the fence — with a boost from Nickel.

Word got out about this unusual bison. Soon Nickel became a celebrity. He appeared on TV newscasts. He was featured in newspapers all over the world. More tourists came to the ranch.

By the following summer they saw a 300 pound buffalo who thought he was a dog. His increasing size played havoc wherever he went.

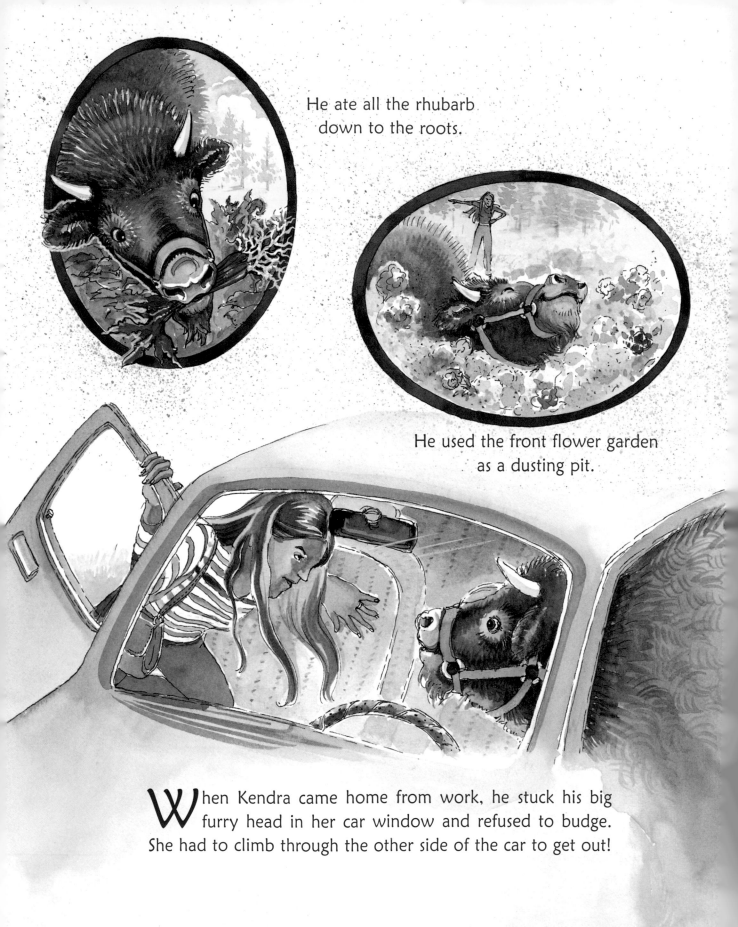

He ate all the rhubarb down to the roots.

He used the front flower garden as a dusting pit.

When Kendra came home from work, he stuck his big furry head in her car window and refused to budge. She had to climb through the other side of the car to get out!

Worst of all, Nickel kept running into things.

Buffalo don't see very well. He often ran into trees while chasing the dogs. One morning Jason stood near the propane tank with his back to Nickel, unaware that the bison was racing toward him, head down. Nickel tossed him into the air and slammed headfirst into the propane tank, while Jason flew over the tank, did three somersaults in the yard and landed on his feet!

During another game of chase, Cruiser and Mickey ran full speed toward the house with Nickel hot on their heels. The dogs dashed through the dog-door and into the house. But Nickel couldn't stop!

"No more buffalo in this house," said Kendra.

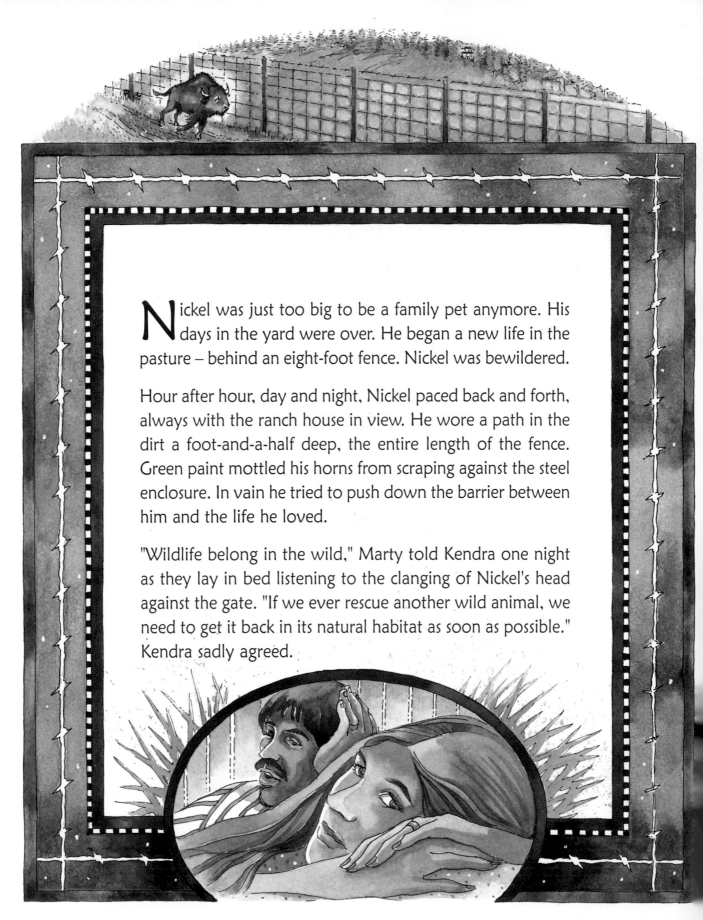

Nickel was just too big to be a family pet anymore. His days in the yard were over. He began a new life in the pasture – behind an eight-foot fence. Nickel was bewildered.

Hour after hour, day and night, Nickel paced back and forth, always with the ranch house in view. He wore a path in the dirt a foot-and-a-half deep, the entire length of the fence. Green paint mottled his horns from scraping against the steel enclosure. In vain he tried to push down the barrier between him and the life he loved.

"Wildlife belong in the wild," Marty told Kendra one night as they lay in bed listening to the clanging of Nickel's head against the gate. "If we ever rescue another wild animal, we need to get it back in its natural habitat as soon as possible." Kendra sadly agreed.

Eventually Nickel adjusted to his life in the pasture. But he remembered a lot from living around humans. He could open any gate that was wired shut, no matter how tightly. Using his horns, Nickel would patiently unfasten the wires until the gate swung open.

Once Nickel joined a party of hikers out for a walk. When they saw a horned buffalo trotting after them, they scampered up the log corners of an old cabin and hung from the roof while one snuck off to get help.

Another time some Native Americans were in a sweat lodge for a special ceremony when Nickel popped in for a visit. Startled, they all dashed for their trucks and nicknamed the intruder, "Big Medicine."

Later Nickel spied Jason fly-fishing at the pond in the pasture. First he ran off with Jason's tackle box. Then he snuck back and took the *rod!*

Other bison share the pasture. There's Daisy, the midget buffalo, Ferdinand the bull, Okie (from Oklahoma), Rawhide and Torrey. Nickel helps Marty care for the herd.

How does Marty move a herd of buffalo? He has Nickel follow his truck, and the rest of the herd follows Nickel through the tunnel beneath the highway.

If aggressive bison threaten Marty, 1400-pound Nickel diverts them away from his friend.

When frightened calves are brought to the ranch, a gentle nudge from Nickel coaxes them out of the truck.

And at spring vaccination time, Nickel leads the herd into the compound, "Elkatraz," for their shots.

ELKATRAZ

When the work is done, there is nothing better than a friendly visit with the neighbors who live nearby.

"Want a cool drink, Nickel?" A neighbor boy offers water from a hose on a hot summer day. Nickel's favorite place is close to the fence greeting the visitors at the park.

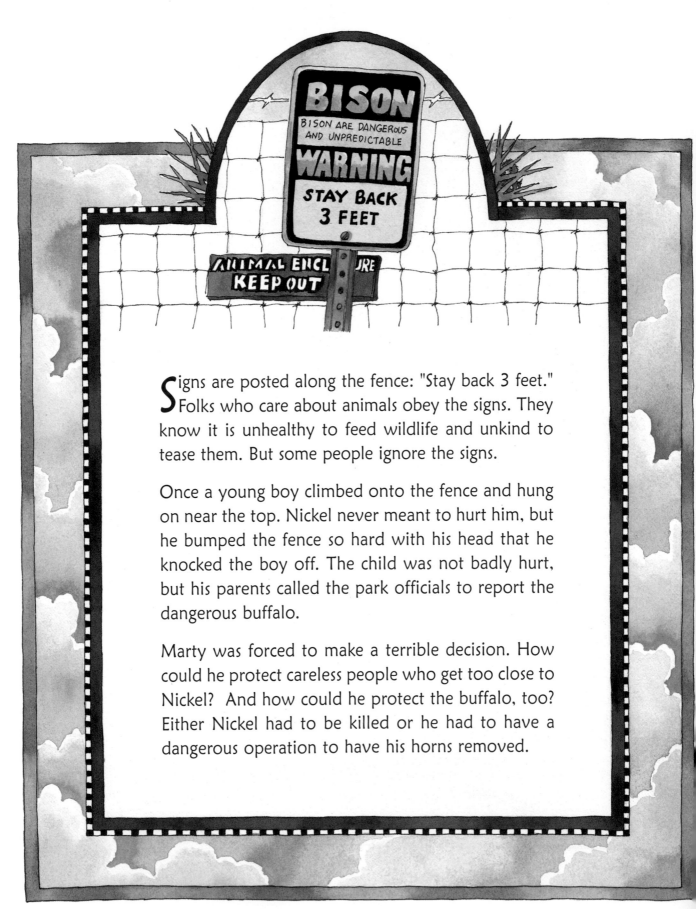

Signs are posted along the fence: "Stay back 3 feet." Folks who care about animals obey the signs. They know it is unhealthy to feed wildlife and unkind to tease them. But some people ignore the signs.

Once a young boy climbed onto the fence and hung on near the top. Nickel never meant to hurt him, but he bumped the fence so hard with his head that he knocked the boy off. The child was not badly hurt, but his parents called the park officials to report the dangerous buffalo.

Marty was forced to make a terrible decision. How could he protect careless people who get too close to Nickel? And how could he protect the buffalo, too? Either Nickel had to be killed or he had to have a dangerous operation to have his horns removed.

Marty could not bear to kill his friend. He had no choice but to remove Nickel's horns.

First the vet gave Nickel an anesthetic to put him to sleep. Then Marty held Nickel's head steady while the horns were sawed off. This left two big open holes. The vet didn't expect Nickel to survive.

Several times each day Marty, Kendra and Jason cleaned the open wounds. Nickel was very depressed for a long time. He lay apart from the herd and away from the fence and the people. Horns are made of bone and never grow back. They are a buffalo's only means of defense.

After several months the wounds finally closed and Nickel got used to the change. He resumed his place close to the fence.

Even without his horns, Nickel continued to help Marty with the herd and have many more adventures.

Every year in the spring a buffalo auction is held at the compound. Most of the year-old heifers, young bulls and older bison are sold. Occasionally a calf will be bought by the zoo or trained for movies and parades. The money from the sale pays for the upkeep of the herd.

Nickel was never sold. By losing his horns he had already paid an enormous price at the hands of humans. He lived the rest of his life at the ranch greeting thousands of people who came to the park to see the bison. Over the years he became famous for his outgoing personality and his attachment to humans. People all over the world remember Nickel, the friendly buffalo.

If you travel west of Denver on I-70, you can visit Nickel's herd.

Stop and say howdy!

History of Nickel's Herd

Millions of buffalo or bison once roamed the North American plains. By the late 1800's bison were almost extinct. In 1902 only 23 wild bison were left in Yellowstone National Park. To increase the Yellowstone herd, the government purchased bison from the Pablo-Allard herd in Montana and from Charles Goodnight in Texas. A few years later in 1913 the Denver Mountain Parks were created. The first land acquired was Genesee Park, in the foothills west of the city. The city's forefathers decided it would be a great attraction to have bison and elk on the land. The government granted permission for bison to be brought from Yellowstone. The bison were shipped by rail to the Denver Stockyards. Then they were transported to Genesee Park in circus wagons. Nickel is descended from these Yellowstone bison. Genesee Park now supports 30 head of bison on 750 acres. Today over 250,000 bison live in parks and ranches throughout North America.

The North American bison is commonly called a buffalo. Bison is the scientific name. Explore Nickel's website for photos, fun activities and a teacher's guide.

www.nickelbuffalo.com

Did you find the 37 squirrels hidden throughout the book?